This sketchbook belongs to:

____

www.ingramcontent.com/pod-product-compliance
Lightning Source LLC
Chambersburg PA
CBHW081822200326
41597CB00023B/4348
9781950263066